ESSENTIAL
MANAGERS

EFFECTIVE
COMMUNICATION

T0005119

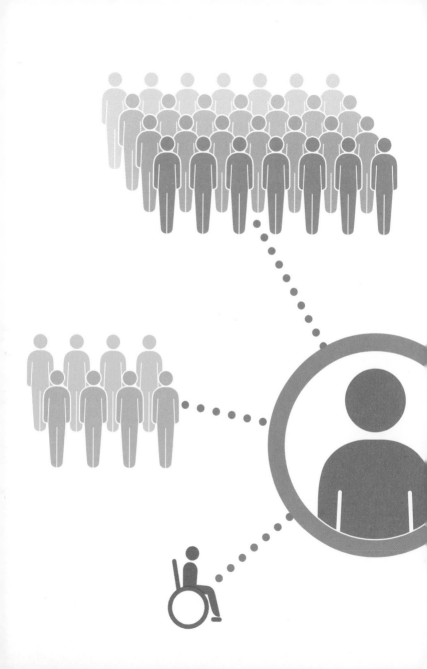

ESSENTIAL
MANAGERS

EFFECTIVE
COMMUNICATION

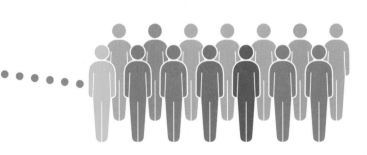

Penguin
Random
House

Produced for DK by Dynamo Ltd
1 Cathedral Court, Southernhay East, Exeter, EX1 1AF

Written by James S. O'Rouke, IV

Senior Art Editor Helen Spencer
Senior Editor Chauney Dunford
US Editor Heather Wilcox
Jacket Design Development Manager Sophia MTT
Jacket Designers Akiko Kato, Juhi Sheth
Producer Nancy-Jane Maun
Production Editor Andy Hilliard
Senior Managing Art Editor Lee Griffiths
Managing Editor Gareth Jones
Associate Publishing Director Liz Wheeler
Art Director Karen Self
Design Director Philip Ormerod
Publishing Director Jonathan Metcalf

This American Edition, 2022
First American Edition, 2009
Published in the United States by DK Publishing
1450 Broadway, Suite 801, New York, NY 10018

Copyright © 2009, 2015, 2022 Dorling Kindersley Limited
DK, a Division of Penguin Random House LLC
22 23 24 25 26 10 9 8 7 6 5 4 3 2 1
001-326977-Apr/2022

A catalog record for this book
is available from the Library of Congress.
ISBN 978-0-7440-5167-4

Printed in China

For the curious
www.dk.com

Contents

Introduction

Communication is, without question, the most valuable skill any manager can possess. It is the link between ideas and action, the process that generates profit. Communication is the emotional glue that binds humans together in relationships, personal and professional. The ability to communicate is what connects people to others in an organization, an industry, and a society. To be skilled at it is to be at the heart of what makes enterprise, private or public, function successfully.

Effective Communication focuses on the processes involved in business communication and concentrates, in particular, on ways in which you can become more effective by becoming more knowledgeable and skilled as a communicator, both in person and remotely. All forms of communication, whether writing, listening, or speaking, are the end products of a process that begins with critical thinking.

This book covers a wide range of topics designed to help you understand the communication process better, from planning a strategy to analyzing your audience. It provides you with guidelines for preparing and delivering an effective speech as well as ideas for expressing yourself on paper. There are tips for dealing with the specific challenges of team communication, including how to run a meeting, give feedback, and resolve conflict. Finally, it gives you ideas for communicating with clients and customers and thinking about your brand and identity. It's all here. The next step is up to you.

Understanding
communication
skills

Communication is more than just a way to get ideas across or exchange points of view. It is the process by which we interact with others and seek information essential to our daily lives, allowing us to control the circumstances in which we work.

01

Defining communication

Think of communication as a process, involving senders and receivers who encode and decode messages that are transmitted by various media and that may be impeded by "noise." The aim of this process is to create a shared understanding in order to generate desired outcomes.

Understanding each other

Humans aren't the only beings who communicate—virtually all forms of life are capable of sending and receiving messages. People, however, are the only living organisms known to communicate not just with signals and signs but through the use of symbols with agreed-upon meanings. If we think about communication as the transfer of meaning, then for each of us, successful communication means

Defining levels of communication

INTRAPERSONAL

Communication **within ourselves,** sending messages to various parts of our bodies, thinking things over, or working silently on a problem.

INTERPERSONAL

Communication **between** or **among people,** sending messages from one person to another—verbally and nonverbally—with the intention of transferring meaning from one person to another.

ORGANIZATIONAL

Communication in the **context of an organization,** sending and receiving messages through various layers of authority and using various channels to discuss topics of interest to the group we belong to or the company we work for.

MASS OR PUBLIC

Sending messages from one person or source to **many people simultaneously,** through the internet, print media, or television.

...hat you will understand something ...st as I do: we are in agreement about ...vhat the sender intended and what the ...eceiver ultimately understood.

Understanding the principles

...ommunication involves a number of ...rinciples, which apply across time ...nd cultures. The process is always:

- **Dynamic** It is constantly undergoing change.
- **Continuous** Even when you hang up the telephone, you're communicating a message that you have nothing more to say.

- **Circular** Communication is rarely entirely one-way. We each take in information from the outside world, determine what it means, and respond.
- **Unrepeatable** Even if we say something again in precisely the same way, our listeners have heard it before and so respond to it differently.
- **Irreversible** We cannot "unsay" words: their effect remains, even if we're asked to disregard them.
- **Complex** We all assign slightly different meanings to words. This variation is a product of our backgrounds, education, and experience and means that there is always the potential for misunderstanding.

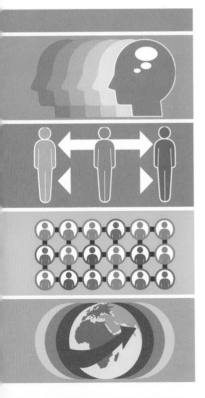

If communication is the **transfer of meaning,** then for successful communication to occur, you should understand something just as I do.

Overcoming barriers

Why do attempts at communication often fail? Broadly speaking, there are two barriers that keep us from communicating successfully: the operations of our bodies and our minds and our assumptions that other people understand and react to the world in the same way that we do.

Unblocking your communications

The information we receive about the world comes from our senses. It is possible, however, for our senses to be impaired or for the source of the message to provide inadequate information to be reliably decoded. In sending messages to others, we must be sensitive to the fact that they may not interpret and experience things in the same way we do.

Overcoming barriers to communication

CONSIDER CULTURE

Be aware that different **backgrounds, education,** and **experience** give people different expectations. Your way of seeing the world is not the only one.

DON'T RUSH TO JUDGE

Never make a judgment **before knowing the facts** about a situation. Acknowledge that you are usually working with incomplete data.

WATCH YOUR LANGUAGE

Recognize that language has **different levels of meaning.** People will respond differently to the same words, especially if the words are vague or general.

CONTROL YOUR FEELINGS

Try to present your message with a cool head—you can appeal to people's emotions, but **don't let yours get the better of you.** Accept that other people may have strong feelings about a subject.

FIGHT STEREOTYPES

Don't assume that all members of a group share the same characteristics. **Put aside any stereotypical views** you may have; treat each person as an individual.

In sending messages to others, we **must be sensitive** to the fact that they may not interpret or experience things **in the same way** that we do.

Ensuring understanding

Communication is more than sending and receiving messages; if the message has been delivered but not understood, no communication has taken place. Everything, from the culture we inhabit to the norms of the groups we belong to, can influence how we perceive the messages, events, and experiences of everyday life. Even individual mindsets, such as unconscious bias, can set up barriers, affecting what we understand and how we react to outside stimuli.

Learn to recognize the barriers likely to block your communications and how you can overcome them. When speaking to someone, for example, monitor their reactions to confirm you are being understood. Remember that the barrier to understanding may lie in the way you have coded your message. Always make the effort to communicate as clearly as possible.

Communicating at work

Communication is a skill that is central to the human experience. We each know how to do it; we've done it since birth and receive additional practice each day. So, why is it so difficult to communicate on the job? As a manager, it is important to understand how the workplace changes the nature of communication for both sender and receiver.

Tailoring your approach

Several factors alter the way we look at communication in the business context. We all have a personal communication style, but within an organization, you often have to adapt your approach to accommodate the needs of those you work with and work for. If you put the preferences of your audience—particularly your boss and your clients—above your own, you will often get what you want faster. The way you communicate also depends on your position within the organization. The higher your level of responsibility, the more you have to take into account when communicating. And as you become more accountable, you need to keep better records—a form of communication to yourself that may later be read by others.

Adapting to your environment

Organizations, like the people who work in them, are in constant flux. Businesses change by necessity with the conditions of the marketplace and the lives of the managers who run them. Your communications must adapt to the conditions in which you find yourself. However, this never constitutes a reason for signing your name to a document that is false or passing along information that you know isn't true.

Matching the culture

All communication must work within an organization's culture. The accepted approach can vary considerably between different organizations: some companies, for example, require every issue to be written in email form and circulated before it can be raised in a team meeting. Other organizations are much more "oral" in nature, offering employees the opportunity to talk things through before writing anything down.

Many companies rely on a particular culture to move day-to-day information through the organization. To succeed in such a business, you must adapt to the existing culture rather than try to change it or ask it to adapt to you.

CHECKLIST...

Adapting your style

	YES	NO
1 Do you understand how the **culture of the organization you work** for affects the way in which you need to communicate?	☐	☐
2 Have you adapted your **writing and speaking style** to the expectations of the culture in which you are working?	☐	☐
3 Have you changed your style to accommodate any changes in the **structure of the company** or the conditions of your industry?	☐	☐
4 Have you noted the communication preferences of your supervisor and **adapted** your **writing, speaking, and listening styles** accordingly?	☐	☐

Planning your approach

Getting people to listen to what you say, read what you write, or look at what you show them isn't easy. How do you persuade them that paying attention to your message is in their best interest? The key to ensuring that your communication hits the mark is detailed planning.

Choosing your approach

The choices you make, from the content of the message you send to the medium you select, all have a direct impact on the outcome of your communication. Whatever the situation, ask yourself about the following:

47%

higher returns to shareholders are **reported** in companies that are led by **good communicators.**

Tip

QUESTION YOUR OWN ROLE

Ask yourself whether you are the **right person** to send the message. Will your signature compel people to action, or might the message be **more effective** coming from your manager or someone closer to the intended audience?

Tip

GET TO KNOW YOUR AUDIENCE
It's all too easy to stereotype an audience, especially when you are working against the clock. Make sure you have **collected all the information** available about your audience and refer to the **key characteristics** as you prepare your speech or document.

Who will receive the message? What is **your relationship** to them? What do they need to know? What **action** do you want them to take?

MESSAGE

What should your message contain? How should your message **impart the information?** Should your message be broad or detailed?

MEDIUM

What's the best way to send this message? Is one medium **quicker** or **cheaper** than another? Will one offer a **better opportunity** for feedback or carry more detail?

CODE

Will your audience understand the words you've used? Will the **words and images** mean the same thing to the audience as they mean to you? Do these words and images have **multiple meanings** for various audiences?

FEEDBACK

How will you know if you've **communicated successfully?** Will the audience response be delayed? Will it be filtered through another source?

NOISE

How many other senders and messages are out there? Whose **message traffic** are you competing with? Will others try to deflect, distort, or disable your communication attempts?

Understanding your audience

Who are these people you're communicating with? What do you know about them? What do they know about you or your subject? How do they feel about it? When preparing to communicate, ask a few simple questions about the people in your audience. Once you know more about them, you can find ways to motivate them to listen.

Assessing your audience is especially important when planning a big public presentation or a report that will be seen by many people. But it is also worth doing to help you better understand those with whom you communicate on a regular basis in your team or company. You don't need to conduct a full-blown assessment every time you talk to or email someone, but knowing what makes people tick will help you get your message across more effectively.

Audience backgrounds

When you're assessing your audience, look for any similarities in personal backgrounds. For example, what is the average age of audience members? Consider whether they will be familiar with the concepts you plan to speak about and the sort of life experiences they may have had. Next, think about the education level of your audience. This will have a significant influence on the content of your talk or document, including its central themes and the vocabulary you employ. The personal beliefs of your audience are an important factor to take into account when planning what you will say. Are they liberal or conservative? What is their political affiliation? Are they committed to a particular religious or social point of view?

In focus

ETHNIC AND GENDER TRAITS
The ethnic origin of members of your audience may be worth knowing, but don't overestimate its value. This information can help you know which issues and positions are of greatest concern to them, but you should not stereotype the views of the members of such a group. Sensitivity to ethnic issues and language styles should be sufficient as you prepare. Similarly, knowing that your audience might be predominantly composed of one gender or another is also of limited benefit. Studies show no statistically significant difference in the responses of professional men and women to a range of stimuli. You would be unwise to assume that you must communicate in one way for men and in another for women.

15%
of the average organization's **collective time** is spent in **meetings.**

Socioeconomic factors

For certain forms of communication, knowing the economic status and lifestyle of your audience is especially important. Gain as much information as you can about the following:

- **Occupation** Knowing how people earn their living will tell you something about their educational background and routines as well as their motivations and interests.
- **Income** Knowing how much money an audience earns can give you some idea of what their concerns are. The less they earn, the more they will be driven by basic needs, such as food and housing. American psychologist Abraham Maslow documented the hierarchy of human needs, showing that higher-level needs—such as self-actualization (the ability to become the best version of yourself)—are only relevant to people once their more basic needs have been met.

- **Socioeconomic status** This term describes where your audience is located in the social/economic spectrum. It is, of course, a direct function of other factors, such as income, education, occupation, neighborhood, friends, family, and more. Think of this as a single descriptor that explains just how much prestige your audience has in the eyes of others in their own society and use it to target your words to address their problems, hopes, and needs.

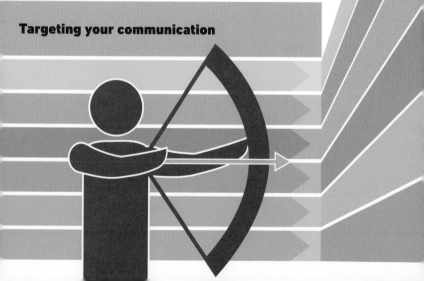

Targeting your communication

WORK WITHIN OBJECTIVES

All of your communication should be **consistent** with and **directly supportive** of the strategic objectives of your organization—its vision, values, and beliefs.

ADAPT TO YOUR AUDIENCE

Appeal to the **basic needs** (such as safety, companionship, or social approval) of your intended audience or their **senses** (use motion, color, and sound). What can you do to hold their attention?

EXPLAIN YOUR POSITION

Use words that your audience will **understand** and concepts they can **relate to.** This means, of course, that you must **know who your audience is** as well as what they know and how they feel about the subject.

MOTIVATE YOUR AUDIENCE

Encourage your audience to accept and act on your message by **appealing to authorities** they respect, the social conformity displayed by others they **know or admire,** the **rationality** of your argument, or their desire to behave in **consistent ways.**

KEEP THEM ON SIDE

Try to prevent your audience from being swayed by other points of view by asking if they are willing to make a **tangible, preferably public, commitment** or reminding them of the benefits to be derived from your approach.

MANAGE EXPECTATIONS

Always let your audience know **what to expect** and **deliver what you promise,** never less. People are disappointed only if their expectations exceed what they actually receive.

Matching the message

Once you know something about the individuals who make up your audience, begin to think about how to approach them. You'll need a strategy to help devise the right message and to choose the most effective method of communication for its recipients.

Hitting the right knowledge level

A thorough knowledge of what your audience already knows about your subject is useful in a number of ways. First, it tells you where to begin. Don't speak down to the audience by explaining fundamentals they already understand. Second, don't start above their heads. Begin at a point they are comfortable with and move on from there.

Managing emotions

Even more important than what the audience knows about your subject is how they feel about it. What they know about taxation is far less relevant than how they feel about it when they listen to a talk about tax reform. You need to tailor your words carefully to what the emotional response of your audience is likely to be. The greater the degree of ego involvement (or emotional response) for a given topic, the narrower the range

Establishing the audience's role

Your message may need to reach only the audience in front of you, or you may be relying on those people to pass on the message to others. Think about everyone who might see or hear your message, including:

PRIMARY AUDIENCE

These are the people who will receive your written or spoken message directly. Make sure that you **understand and address** their needs, interests, and concerns.

SECONDARY AUDIENCE

Others might read or **hear of your message indirectly.** Could the communication be given to a reporter, union organizer, competitor, or go viral on social media?

GETTING YOUR MESSAGE ACROSS

Do's	Don'ts
O **Know as much as you can about who will read or hear your words.**	O Assume the audience knows all or nothing about your subject.
O **Tailor your message to the needs and interests of your audience.**	O Act as if the audience already shares your ideas and interests.
O **Understand who the key decision makers are and their criteria for making decisions.**	O Fail to check who exactly is in your audience and what they need to know in order to act.
O **Know who is respected by your audience and seek their approval for what you recommend.**	O Assume your ideas are good enough to stand up on their own and not discuss them.

f acceptable positions open to you. n other words, people are much more open-minded on topics they are ndifferent about than they are on topics hey care about passionately. If you misjudge an emotional response, our communication will fail.

Tailor your words carefully to what the **emotional response** of your **audience** is likely to be.

GATEKEEPERS

These are the people or platforms you have to **route your message** through and that might filter, block, leak, distort, or amplify it. Does something stand between you and the audience you hope to reach?

OPINION LEADERS

These are individuals who have **significant influence** over members of the audience. Who do they admire or listen to on this subject? How could they react to your message?

KEY DECISION MAKERS

These are people with the **power to influence** the outcome of the communication.

Choosing your medium

Most managers make decisions about whether to write or speak to someone based on two criteria: convenience and their own personal preferences. But an effective choice of communication medium or channel depends on much more than what suits you at the time.

Learning to ignore instinct

Many managers choose a form of communication instinctively, and not always for the right reasons. For example, if you need to give bad news to a colleague but don't want to provoke a confrontation, you might choose to send an email, even though your colleague would prefer to hear from you in person. On another occasion, you might choose to make a phone or video call rather than write a letter because it seems quicker or easier.

You might make this choice even when the message is complex and would benefit from extensive explanation, detailed description, or visual aids. In fact, just two factors should govern your choice of medium for any message. You should think first about the preferences of the person or audience receiving your message and second about the characteristics and benefits of speaking versus those of writing.

When to write

Writing produces a **permanent record,** can convey great detail, is often more precise, and can be used for careful wording. If it's important that you say something in an exact way, write it down. Because writing allows you to interpret information in your own time, it can also help reduce miscommunications with those who do not share the same first language as you. And, of course, if your audience likes source material or **lots of detail,** such as large lists, you can provide that as an appendix or attachment.

Keep in mind that you may have to share your message with many people, and it may be impractical to speak to each of them. Writing in a **precise, persuasive** way may be the best approach to influence your audience.

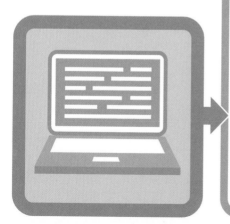

THE PLATINUM RULE

We're all familiar with the old rule: "Do unto others as you would have them do unto you." It's a good rule, but it contains a small flaw. What if others don't want to receive the same treatment as you? What if their preferences are, in fact, significantly different? The Platinum Rule, devised by communication expert Tony Alessandra, who has advised companies such as Apple, Ford, and IBM, is a variation of that age-old maxim: "Do unto others as they want to be done unto." This means treat others as they want to be treated, not how you think they should be treated. Communicate with others in the manner that they prefer, and you'll get what you want: their time, attention, and cooperation.

When to speak

Speaking provides a **richer context**—it includes the use of nonverbal cues and allows for more emotion. It is **less rigid,** as it leaves no permanent record, and may also be much quicker.

Speaking to others also **invites their participation.** It may be the best way to elicit ideas, size up other people's feelings, and even discover any possible objections to your message before decisions have been made and formalized in writing. Once something is written down, people tend to feel committed to that course of action, even if the documents can easily be revised. A conversation or discussion, on the other hand, has a more transitory feel to it: it is **flowing and flexible** and less permanent and formal than written forms of communication.

TRY MESSAGING

A mix of writing and speech, **instant messaging** is faster than email but still allows you to be precise, be detailed, and chat with multiple people. Use it to **swap documents** or **talk through ideas.**

Speaking
and writing

Two of the most important skills for a manager, and often also the most daunting, are to stand up in front of an audience and deliver a presentation and to communicate effectively in writing, whether in formal business letters, email correspondence, or detailed reports. For both, clear thinking, preparation, and practice are the keys to success.

02

Planning your speech

Preparing for a business presentation is the most important stage of the process. While it may seem daunting at first, planning your speech becomes much easier once you break the task down into manageable steps, ensuring that you address all the relevant issues at the right time

Defining substance and style

When it comes to giving a speech, content is king. Substance matters, and there is absolutely no substitute for knowing what you're talking about. This means that, whenever possible, you should select a topic that you know and understand, so that you can talk about it with confidence. However, this also depends on your audience; never forget that they are the reason you are giving the speech. Using your knowledge of your audience to tailor the content to meet their expectations is not a guarantee of success, but it is certainly a step in the right direction.

> Identifying your **role** as a speaker and your **importance** to the listeners is essential.

Determining your purpose

Before you start to plan the details of your speech, make sure that you know why you are speaking. If you can't come up with a reason for speaking, then don't speak. Identifying your role as a speaker and your importance to the listeners is especially important. It may be that this audience wants your views on the subject at hand and is keenly interested in your opinions. Alternatively, your purpose may be purely to inform them about a topic, and the demand for your opinions may not be as high as you imagine.

Also, find out all you can about the context in which the presentation will take place. You need to know the answers to questions such as is your audience still in the fact-gathering stage, or are they ready to make a decision? What is their reason for listening to you? How urgent is the subject you'll be speaking about? Have recent events, either locally or globally, affected their view of the topic in any way? Are your listeners involved in a process that will require them to take action after hearing what you have to say?

Tip

MAKE TIME FOR RESEARCH
Delivering the speech is the **main goal,** but success only comes through careful preparation. **Remember the 80:20 rule**—spend about 80 percent of your time on **research and preparation,** and only around 20 percent on **practice and delivery.**

Case study

PREPARING TO SUCCEED

Elizabeth Allen, chief communications officer of the international office supplies firm Staples, Inc., was given the task of drafting a press-conference speech for her CEO, Tom Stemberg, to announce Staples's sponsorship of a new sports arena in Los Angeles. Ms. Allen knew that this financial arrangement would be covered by the sports press, not the business press. She also knew that sports figures, civic officials, investors, and reporters would be in the room: "Many people thought the name would be a local, Californian company . . . This was a Boston company putting its name on a Los Angeles landmark. There were cultural factors at work here, as well as political and business factors." As she considered how to prepare the speech, she decided three things: she would reduce her thinking to one or two main points; she would include a few examples and anecdotes that the local audience would relate to; and, most importantly, she would cite at least one powerful reason why the relationship between her company and the city of Los Angeles would be productive and long-term.

Preparing your speech

Once you have a clear picture in your mind of why you are giving the presentation, who your audience is, and what they want to hear from you, start to make a detailed plan of your speech. This planning stage is vital, so make sure that you don't leave it to the last minute. You need to be completely familiar with the structure and content of your speech by the time you deliver it. There are eight key steps to preparing a successful presentation.

Steps to preparing a speech

01

COMPOSE A THESIS STATEMENT

Write a **one-sentence declaration** of what you want the audience to **know, understand, believe,** or **do.** Make it brief, simple, comprehensive, and as complete as possible.

02

DEVELOP THE MAIN POINTS

Restrict yourself to just **two or three main points,** so that you will have time to explain and support them all. Make sure that all of your **evidence** relates to and is supportive of your principal reason for speaking.

03

GATHER SUPPORTING MATERIALS

Now, gather evidence to support your main points. Use your knowledge of the audience to select the kinds of proof that they will find **most convincing.** Make your evidence **compelling, recent,** and fully **transparent** to your listeners.

04

THINK ABOUT STRUCTURE

Consider the order in which you will **deliver the information** and think about what you will say in your **introduction,** in the **body** of the speech, and in your **conclusion.**

|05

PREPARE YOUR OUTLINE

Write a one-page outline of your speech. Think about the **issues** you plan to raise, the **sequence** in which you will address each of them, and the **evidence** you'll offer your audience in support of those ideas.

You must be **completely familiar** with both the structure and the **content** of your **speech** by the time you **deliver** it.

|06

CONSIDER VISUALS

Think about what visuals will best enhance your speech, by helping **explain, reinforce,** and **clarify your main points.** Sometimes, it is easier to show the audience something than to say it.

|07

WRITE THE SPEECH

Now, prepare the content of your speech in detail. Some people choose to write in **short bullet points;** others write their **script** out more fully. Choose the way that best suits you, but remember that your audience wants to hear you **speak to them,** not read to them.

Make sure that all of your **evidence relates to** and is **supportive** of your principal **reason for speaking.**

|08

PREPARE YOUR NOTES

Finally, transfer your speech into the **notes you will use to deliver it.** These may be lines on a PowerPoint presentation, written notes on note cards, or the full manuscript.

Developing visual support

Behavioral scientists have known for many years that visual images can have a powerful effect on the process of learning. In some cases, pictures may reach people who simply don't listen well to the spoken word or who may not understand what the words mean.

How does visual support help?

Behavioral scientists have found that visual support is important in communication for three main reasons:

- It can help explain, reinforce, and clarify the spoken word during a presentation. If you can't say something easily, you may be able to show it to your audience.
- People tend to recognize ideas most easily when they are presented as a combination of both words and pictures rather than when presented as either words or pictures alone.
- Some people pay more attention to what they see than what they hear and can more quickly and easily recall information and concepts with a visual component than those that are just spoken aloud.

89%

of people use Microsoft's **PowerPoint** software to create their **presentations.**

Choosing when to use it

Displaying information in a visual manner will enhance most presentations but tends to work best:

O When you have new data for your audience

O When the information you hope to convey is complex or technical in nature

O If your message is coming to the audience in a new context

O For certain types of information—such as numbers, quick facts, quotes, and lists

O For explaining relationships or comparisons

O For revealing geographical or spatial patterns

Tip

CHOOSE THE RIGHT CHART

Charts and graphs are a useful way to display data. Be sure to select the type of chart (such as a pie chart, bar chart, or line graph) that **most clearly illustrates** any comparisons you want to make and use color carefully to **emphasize your point.**

Visual support can help **explain, reinforce,** and **clarify** the spoken word: try **showing as well as telling.**

Using visuals effectively

Good visuals have a number of characteristics in common. The most important is simplicity. The more complex a visual display becomes, the more difficult it is for an audience to understand. Keep your visuals clear, ordered, and simple when trying to explain an important idea or relationship.

Good visuals use color to explain and attract. Very few people tend to have exactly the same taste in colors, but almost everyone appreciates occasions when colors are used meaningfully and consistently. Certain traditions, such as using red numbers or bars to indicate a loss and black ones to indicate profit, allow audiences to quickly grasp information. Try using a simple legend to explain color use on your charts and graphs; it helps the audience and will ensure consistency and simplicity in your visual aids.

> Keep your visuals **clear** and **simple** when trying to explain an **important idea.**

Using visuals well

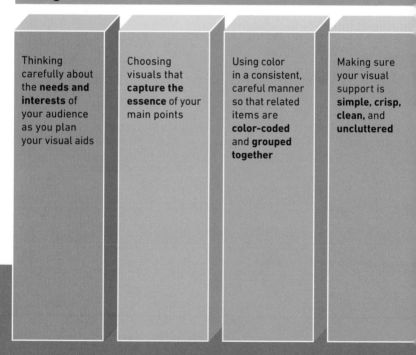

Thinking carefully about the **needs and interests** of your audience as you plan your visual aids

Choosing visuals that **capture the essence** of your main points

Using color in a consistent, careful manner so that related items are **color-coded** and **grouped together**

Making sure your visual support is **simple, crisp, clean,** and **uncluttered**

Tip

Although you should respect your company's **brand guidelines,** you don't have to be a slave to corporate PowerPoint or Google Slides templates if they result in dull, predictable visuals. Try experimenting with **novel presentation software,** such as Prezi, or make your own slides using your preferred graphics software and save them in a standard format, such as PDF.

3

seconds is the maximum time it should take to **understand** a **slide.**

Limiting the amount of text alongside your visuals to a few key words: this will produce **a more powerful message** than wordy slides

Avoiding generic or "stock" images and visuals that are only indirectly related to your main points

Building up a **personal library of images,** symbols, and graphics to enhance your messages

On important occasions, using a **professional graphic designer** to create a polished presentation

Improving your confidence

It's one thing to know your material. It's another matter entirely to believe that you can confidently speak on stage or present remotely to a group of strangers. Understanding your message and having a well-organized speech are important to your success, but so is self-confidence.

Improving your delivery

Rehearsal will help improve your speech and raise your level of self-confidence. Simply knowing that you've been through the contents of your speech more than once builds familiarity and is reassuring. It will also ensure you talk for the correct amount of time. A run-through or two will show whether you have too much, too little, or just enough to say. Rehearsal will also help you improve your transitions. By practicing your speech, you'll be able to identify the rough spots and work on smoothing the transition from one point to another and from one part of the speech to another.

Using notes

The best speakers seem to confidently deliver their speeches extemporaneously, or "from the heart," without notes. Such speeches aren't really memorized word-for-word but rather are thoroughly researched, well rehearsed, and professionally supported. Many extemporaneous speakers will use

> **Tip**
>
> **KEEP NOTES SIMPLE**
> Losing your place in lengthy notes can give your **confidence** a serious hit, so make sure your notes are **quick and easy to use,** giving you the information you need at a glance.

their visual support—usually digital slides prepared using presentation software—to prompt their memories. Others prefer to use note cards or the full manuscript. Whichever you choose, make sure that your notes are simple, are easy to follow, and allow you to maintain eye contact with the audience.

CHECKLIST...
Being prepared
YES   NO

1 Have you double-checked the **time and location** for your speech? .... ☐ ☐

2 Are you sure about the **length of time** allotted to the speech? .... ☐ ☐

3 Have you decided how to **arrange the room**? .... ☐ ☐

4 Have you found out whether you are **using a podium** or are free to walk around the room during the speech? .... ☐ ☐

5 Have you tested the **microphone** and **sound system**? .... ☐ ☐

6 Are you familiar with the **arrangements** and **systems** for visuals? .... ☐ ☐

7 Do you know what **lighting is available,** and have you determined whether it needs to change for **screen visuals** or handouts during your talk? .... ☐ ☐

8 If you are presenting remotely, are you familiar with the platform you are using? .... ☐ ☐

Gaining confidence

The better prepared you are, the more secure you will feel. Think about all aspects of your presentation, from the software and microphone that you will be using to your video-chat backdrop or the layout of the conference room. The knowledge that you have arranged every detail and carefully planned and rehearsed your talk will build your confidence. If you get cold feet, remember that you've been asked to speak because the audience is interested in your expertise and viewpoint. Trust in your ability and intelligence to deliver an effective speech.

Delivering your speech

You've researched the topic thoroughly, written and organized your thoughts, and rehearsed using your visuals. Use the confidence that you've developed in planning and rehearsal to take the next step: get up and speak. You are the medium, or bearer, of the message, and your delivery is critical to the successful communication of your ideas.

Improving your delivery

As you approach the challenge of becoming an accomplished public speaker, keep in mind that no one is born with great public-speaking ability. Language is the habit of a lifetime, and your ability to speak with conviction and sincerity is a function of your willingness to work at it. Your skills will improve with every speech that you make, and as you master the art of presentation, chances are that others in a position of influence will notice and reward you for your effort.

> Your ability to speak with **conviction** and **sincerity** is a function of your willingness to **work at it.**

In focus

PRESENTING VIRTUALLY

There are a few extra things to consider when delivering a speech virtually. Before you begin, check your camera, microphone, internet connection, and backdrop and that you are comfortable using your software. Turn off notifications on your device and let anyone nearby know they must not disturb you. Because your audience can't see as many of your gestures as they can in person, it's a good idea to exaggerate your body language a little and talk more animatedly and slowly; also, try bringing your hands into frame. Sit directly facing the camera and feel free to share your screen, but don't forget to switch back to your face between slides. Asking your audience to turn their own cameras on can help you gauge their interest and adapt accordingly. Above all, though, smile, sit up straight, and engage.

Ways to keep your audience interested

MAKE A CONNECTION

Prepare yourself: breathe deeply, smile, think positively, and speak

Humanize and personalize your speech—share your experiences, values, goals, and fears

Do your best to be one of them (unless it's clear you are not)

Use humor where appropriate (unless you are not funny)

Actively involve the audience as much as you can

Focus on current local events and issues known to the audience

HELP THEM UNDERSTAND

Blueprint the speech: tell the audience where your talk is going

Begin with the familiar and then move to the unfamiliar

Talk process first and then add in the detail

Visualize and demonstrate your ideas where you can

Summarize your key points as you progress through a speech

Give examples to illustrate your concepts and ideas

Tell stories and dramatize your central theme

Use the **confidence** that you've developed in **planning** and **rehearsal** to take the next step: **get up and speak.**

Becoming a better writer

Very few people think writing is easy. Good writing—that is, writing with power, grace, dignity, and impact—takes time, careful thought, and revision. Such writing is often the product of many years of training and practice. Even though writing may sometimes seem like hard work, with practice, you can learn to do it well.

Organizing your writing

Good business writing is simple, clear, and concise. By not calling attention to itself, good writing is "transparent," helping the reader focus on the idea you are trying to communicate rather than on the words that you are using to describe it.

The key to good business writing is organization. You need to know where you are going before you start, so do your research and identify the key issues you need to cover. Compose a list of the most important points and use them to create an outline. If your document will include an overview section containing your purpose for writing, write this first. Next, tackle the most important paragraphs before filling out the details and any supplementary material.

Have I "translated" any **technical terms?**

Have I explained adequately?

Does my writing **flow in a logical way,** and have I given **complex explanations** in a step-by-step form?

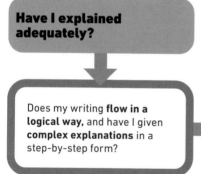

Use **simple**, **down-to-earth** words and avoid needless ones and wordy expressions.

Writing for clarity

When composing an email, letter, or report, keep in mind that your reader often doesn't have much time: senior managers, in particular, generally have tight schedules and too much to read. They need your written communication to quickly and clearly give them the details they need to know.

Ensure that your writing style is both precise and concise. Use simple, down-to-earth words and avoid needless ones and wordy expressions. Simple words and expressions are more quickly understood and can add power to your ideas. Be direct and avoid vague terms, such as "very" and "slightly"; this will show that you have confidence in what you are saying and will add power to your ideas. Make sure, too, that everything you write is grammatically correct—you don't want your busy reader to have to reread your sentences to try to decipher their meaning.

Keep your paragraphs short; they are more inviting and more likely to get read. If your document must include numbers, use them with restraint—a paragraph filled with numbers can be difficult to read and follow. Use a few numbers selectively to make your point and then put the rest in tables and graphics.

Have I said enough to **answer questions** and **allay fears** without giving too much detail?

Have I used **visuals** to help explain **complex facts?**

Have I cautioned the reader, where necessary, against **common mistakes** and **misreading** of the information?

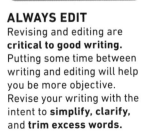

81%

of **businesspeople** agree that **poorly written** material **wastes** a lot of their **time.**

Tip

ALWAYS EDIT
Revising and editing are **critical to good writing.** Putting some time between writing and editing will help you be more objective. Revise your writing with the intent to **simplify, clarify,** and **trim excess words.**

Making your writing come alive

To escape from outdated, excessively formal writing styles, try to make your writing more like your speaking and then "tidy it up." Imagine your reader is in front of you—how would you explain things to them? Write your words down, aiming to make them as clear, fresh, and easy to read as possible. You may need to write a first draft for structural purposes and then go back over your document.

Make sure that your writing is:

VIGOROUS AND DIRECT

Use **active sentences** and avoid the passive voice. Be **more definite** by limiting the use of the word "not."

In focus

THE RIGHT ORDER

A poorly organized document reads like a mystery story. Clue by clue, it unfolds details that make sense only toward the end—if the reader gets that far. Your job is to make it easier for the reader, by explaining each point with an overview, followed by details. To avoid any confusion, always give directions before reasons, requests before justifications, answers before explanations, conclusions before details, and solutions before problems. Try the approach used in many news stories. They start with the most important information and taper off to the least important.

Tip

MAKE IT PERFECT

Eliminate factual errors, typos, misspellings, bad grammar, and incorrect punctuation in your writing. Remember that if **too many details** in an email you have written are recognized to be incorrect, your entire line of thinking may be considered suspect.

CONNECTING WITH THE READER

Reach out to your reader by occasionally using questions. A request **gains emphasis** when it ends with a question mark. Rather than writing, "Please advise as to whether the meeting is still scheduled for February 21," simply ask: "Is the meeting still scheduled for February 21?"

MADE UP OF SHORT SENTENCES

This won't guarantee clarity, but short sentences will prevent many of the confusions that can easily occur in longer ones. Try the ear test: **read your writing aloud** and break apart any sentence you can't finish in one breath.

FREE OF CLICHÉS AND JARGON

Tired **words and expressions** make your writing appear superficial.

Imagine your reader is in **front** of you—**think** how you would **explain** things to them and **write** your words down.

Meeting your reader's needs

Before you write, find out what the reader expects, wants, and needs. If you later discover that you must deviate from these guidelines, let the reader know why. When composing your document, don't include material that you don't need: you may be accused of missing the point. Make sure, too, that you always separate facts from opinions in your writing. The reader should never be in doubt as to what you know to be true and what you think may be the case. Always apply a consistent approach to avoid misunderstandings.

Capturing and keeping your readers' attention

USE CONTRACTIONS

Make your writing softer and more accessible by occasionally using the contractions that we naturally speak with, such as "I'm," "we're," "you'd," "they've," "can't," "don't," and "let's."

ALLOW SENTENCES TO END WITH A PREPOSITION

Don't reword a sentence just to move a preposition (e.g., "after," "at," "by," "from," "of," "to," or "up") from the end. You are likely to lengthen, tangle, and stiffen the sentence.

WRITE WITH PERSONAL PRONOUNS

Use "we," "us," and "our" when speaking for the company. Use "I," "me," and "my" when speaking for yourself. Either way, be generous with the use of the word "you."

USE THE PRESENT TENSE WHENEVER POSSIBLE

This adds immediacy to your writing. Be careful, however, not to slip from the present to the past tense and back again, as this will make your writing confusing. Select one tense and stick to it.

Find out what your reader **expects, wants,** and **needs:** if you deviate from this in your writing, **let the reader know why.**

USE SHORT TRANSITIONS

Use "but" more than "however" and "more than" rather than "in addition to." Use more formal transitions only for variety. Don't be afraid to start a sentence with words like "but," "so," "yet," "and," or "or."

Writing a business letter

Business letters are primarily external documents, although managers will occasionally use letters to correspond with subordinates and executives within their organization. Good letters are crisp, concise, and organized so that readers can follow and understand the content with little effort.

Writing successful letters

Although most business correspondence is conducted by email and messaging these days, physical letters still have their place in the workplace (unless your company runs a paperless office). Often seen as carrying more weight than electronic messages, business letters are good for communicating formal, especially legal matters, where it is important that your recipient gets a hard copy of your correspondence. These include contractual issues and policy changes, disciplinary proceedings and commendations, and resignations, but business letters can be used to convey almost any important issue.

Your success as a business writer depends, in large part, on your ability to convince others that what you have written is worth their attention. This is more likely if your letter meets three

criteria: it should be concise, it should be clear, and it absolutely must be organized. Be careful, however. Brevity is desirable, but you can overdo it. Avoid being too brief or curt and make sure that your reader has enough information to understand the subject. Include each issue relevant to the subject and explain the process, the outcome, or the decision to the satisfaction of the reader. If you were receiving the letter, would the information be sufficient? Would you be satisfied that the writer had taken you seriously?

> **Tip**
>
> **GET ATTACHED**
> You don't always have to send business letters **by mail**—remember, you can also **attach** them to an **email** as a **text or PDF** document. The recipient won't have a hard copy of your document, but they will have something they can easily **print or archive** that arrives much **faster.**

Showing interest

When responding to a letter you have received, aim to show that you are genuinely interested. The sender thought the issue was important enough to write about; you should think so too. Show by your words and actions that you care about them and the contents of the letter.

Give everyone the benefit of the doubt. If something in a letter seems off, try to put yourself in the writer's shoes.

Maybe they wrote it because they have different information or simply made a mistake. Never write and quickly send off an angry letter. Venting may make you feel good, but it's almost never a good idea to post a hostile reply. Take your time and cool down before you compose an angry letter. Then, wait until the following day to reread it. Chances are, you'll think twice before sending.

Hitting the right tone

If you have to deliver bad news by letter, say you are sorry. Use phrases such as, "I am sorry to say that . . ." or "I regret to say that we'll be unable to [do something] because . . ." to soften the blow. If your reader thinks you don't care, you may spark an unwanted reaction. If you have good news, say you are glad: "I am delighted to tell you that . . ." Alternatively, use a phrase such as "You will be pleased to learn that . . ."

A letter should be **clear** and **organized.** Brevity is desirable, but you can overdo it: make absolutely sure that your reader has enough information to **understand the subject.**

In focus

FORM LETTERS

Form letters are standardized letters on regularly occurring topics designed to be sent to multiple recipients. While such a "one-size-fits-all" approach may be tempting, it is usually a recipe for disaster. A letter must answer all the questions its audience is likely to have, responding to their fears, doubts, and concerns. In situations in which it is absolutely necessary to use a form letter, test market your efforts by showing them to several present or past members of the audience and asking for suggestions for improvement.

Using email and instant messaging effectively

Email is now the key means of staying in touch, sharing data and graphics, and managing the flow of information needed to run a business. Text, or SMS, messaging, when properly managed, can also be become a productivity booster; a direct, interactive link to customers; and an essential tool to communicate with other staff.

Reducing your emailing time

Email is a tool; don't let it become your master. Limit the time you spend on email by following these tips:

- **Send less, get less** Think carefully about whether you really need to draft new messages or respond to those you've already received.
- **Escape the endless reply loop** Silence in response to an email message may feel rude but is acceptable. If you wish to reassure someone that no reply is necessary, finish a message with "no reply needed" or a request with "Thanks in advance." Avoid asking any questions for which you don't really want or need answers.
- **Think twice about the "cc" box** If you copy a large number of people on your emails, and they all respond with a reply that needs an answer, you may create unnecessary traffic.

Sending better emails

@

1

Pick the subject line of the email carefully: make it informative and brief so the recipient can easily find and act on it.

4

Be careful with criticism: be sure to provide enough context and background to avoid a misunderstanding.

5

Keep it short. If you need more than a few paragraphs, send as an attachment or consider if the matter could be better addressed over the phone.

CHECKLIST...
Knowing when email is inappropriate

	YES	NO
1 Do I need to **convey or discern emotion?**	☐	☐
2 Do I need to **cut through** the communication clutter?	☐	☐
3 Do I need to **move quickly?**	☐	☐
4 Do I want a remote communication **to be secure?**	☐	☐
5 Am I trying to **reach someone** who doesn't have access to (or check) email?	☐	☐
6 Do I want to **engage people** and get an **immediate response?**	☐	☐

> Be sparing in your use of email: think very carefully about whether you really need to **draft new messages** or respond to those you've **already received.**

2

Now, **write the main body** of the email, using correct grammar, punctuation, and capitalization.

3

Avoid abbreviations and cyberjargon: most business professionals dislike them. WIDLTO (when in doubt, leave them out).

6

Use a signature to conclude your email, but keep it simple: don't be tempted to add humorous or "inspiring" quotes.

7

Before you send the email, **check your attachments.** Send only those that your recipient needs or wants to see.

Developing good email habits

Don't check your email constantly. Check it at regular intervals—hourly, or even just three times a day, if your work is less deadline-driven. Be disciplined about email management. Aim to handle each message just once. If it's unimportant or irrelevant, hit the delete key. If you spend more than three hours a week sorting through irrelevant mail, you have a problem. If a message is something you'll need to respond to, decide whether to do it now or later, when you will have the time and information you need. Don't put pressure on others by sending emails after hours. Wait until the next day or make it clear that you don't expect an answer right away.

Consider if you are posting to the right people on the right channel—if they don't need to be in chat, don't add them

Ask yourself if instant messaging is the right medium for your message—don't use it for formal matters

How to use instant messaging (IM)

In focus

INTRANETS

Intranets (private company networks) are great for facilitating two-way communication between staff and management and among employees. They can also provide access to company knowledge, such as statistics and best practice documents, and enhance collaboration. Many integrate with third-party apps and incorporate social media–style features too.

Write clearly, explain any jargon, and avoid slang—it may not be appropriate or translate well

Instant messaging apps are great for **talking through** issues at a **distance** and getting documents in a **hurry.**

Check the recipient's status —respect their right to set it to "away" or "busy"

Don't pressure people to respond at once—they might be busy or on a break

Messaging and texting

Instant messaging has become a popular workplace tool, allowing groups of two, three, or even hundreds of people to connect and receive responses instantly. Apps, such as Slack and Microsoft Teams, are great for talking through issues at a distance and getting documents in a hurry. But such immediacy also requires new considerations regarding etiquette and expectations (see graphic). Set your status to "away" or "busy" to reduce distractions.

Using text messages to reach out to customers is established practice in many businesses, but few firms use texts for other types of communications. However, they are an ideal medium for alerts, such as notifications of downtime of computer servers, and for simple company announcements, such as motivational messages and new employee introductions.

Writing reports

Reports are longer and more comprehensive than most documents and are written for the purpose of documenting actions, describing projects and events, and capturing information on complex issues. They are often written by more than one person for audiences with multiple needs and interests.

Planning your report

There are three main questions to consider when compiling a report:

- **Who is in your audience?** Think about their level of interest in the content and their familiarity with the issues, ideas, and vocabulary you plan to use.
- **What is the ideal format?** Consider how your readers will use the document—will they start from the beginning and read through page by page, or will they skip to sections that interest them most?
- **Is the document properly organized?** Consider using a bold typeface for headings and subheadings to help organize the information and make it retrievable.

> Busy business leaders may only read the **executive summary** of a report, so it must tell them all they need to know in order for them to **understand** your recommendations.

Tip

INCLUDE A COVER LETTER

As a courtesy to your reader, always include a cover letter or email to accompany the report, explaining **what the document covers and why.** Where appropriate, include the report's most **important recommendations** or **findings.**

Writing the report

Reports are divided into three sections: front matter (including title page, abstract, table of contents, and list of figures and tables), the main body of the report, and end matter (bibliography, appendices, glossary, and index). Begin the main body with an executive summary, detailing the report's key points and recommendations. Busy executives may only read this section, so it must tell them all they need to know in order for them to agree with your recommendations.

Dividing your report into sections

SECTION	CONTENT
TITLE PAGE	A single page containing the full title of the report, the names of the authors, the date of issue, and the name of the organization to which the report is submitted.
ABSTRACT	A paragraph that summarizes the major points. It enables a reader to decide whether to read the entire work.
TABLE OF CONTENTS	A list of all the headings within the report in the order of their appearance, along with a page number for each.
LIST OF FIGURES AND TABLES	Reports with more than five figures or tables should include a page listing each one with its page number.
FOREWORD (OPTIONAL)	An introductory statement usually written by an authority figure. It provides background information and places the report in the context of other works in the field.
PREFACE (OPTIONAL)	This describes the purpose, background, or scope of the report.
EXECUTIVE SUMMARY	This provides more information than the abstract and enables readers to scan the report's primary points. These summaries are usually restricted to a few pages.
MAIN TEXT	This forms the main body of the report and explains your work and its findings.
CONCLUSION	This contains not only concluding remarks but also any recommended actions for the readers.
BIBLIOGRAPHY	A listing of all the sources consulted to prepare the report; it may also suggest additional reading and resources.
APPENDICES	Information that supplements the main report as evidence, such as lists, tables of figures, and charts and graphs.
GLOSSARY	An alphabetical list of definitions of unusual terms used.
INDEX	An alphabetical list of topics with page numbers.

Communicating
with your team

A team is only as good as its communication;
misunderstandings can cause a huge amount of
extra work and lost time. When managing a team,
focus on giving constructive feedback, briefing
thoroughly, and dealing effectively with conflict.

03

Listening effectively

Good communication is not just about getting your point across. It's also about staying quiet and listening to what others have to say. As a manager, listening actively and understanding your colleagues are at the heart of creating a team that performs to the best of its ability.

Learning when to listen

Listening is a skill you acquire naturally but can improve upon if you're motivated to do so. The first step toward becoming a better listener is, surprisingly, to stop: you need to stop talking, stop trying to carry on more than one conversation, and stop interrupting. Let the other person speak. As others are talking, allow yourself to respond cognitively and emotionally, taking in the factual information and the tone of their remarks, without responding. Then, ask carefully thought-out questions that will clarify what they have said and reassure you of its basis in fact.

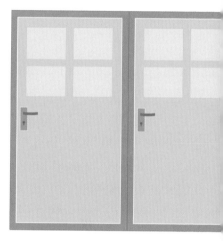

Tip

LISTENING REMOTELY
Because you can't pick up on as many nonverbal cues, actively listening when working remotely requires more focus. Listen in a **quiet place** and tell others not to disturb you. On video calls, **mute your mic** when not speaking and **watch the screen** to ensure you're taking everything in.

25%

of **corporate leaders** have a **listening deficit,** according to **feedback** from their colleagues.

Getting the message

Start by trying to see things from the speaker's point of view and let your actions demonstrate this. Show interest with your body language: look the speaker in the eyes and maintain an open and nonthreatening posture. Give the speaker physical signs of your undivided attention: close the door, hold your calls, and put aside whatever you're working on.

Listen carefully to how something is said: look out for hints of sarcasm, cynicism, or irony in what you hear. Try to tune in to the speaker's mood and intention. Communication is a shared responsibility, so it is up to you to ensure that you understand the message.

Once you have listened to what a person has to say and clarified anything you're not sure of, evaluate the facts and evidence. Ask yourself if the evidence is recent, reliable, accurate, and relevant.

Tip

WATCH WHAT YOU HEAR
Just because you want to hear something doesn't mean it is what the speaker is **really saying.** Avoid falling into the trap of **selective hearing.**

LISTENING ACTIVELY

Do's

- O **Listen regularly to difficult material to hone your listening ability.**

- O **Give your full and undivided attention to the speaker.**

- O **Listen to the argument in the speaker's terms and in the order he or she wishes to follow.**

- O **Focus on the reasons for the speaker's approach and discussion.**

Don'ts

- O Assume that everything interesting should be provided in written form.

- O Pretend to listen while actually doing something else.

- O Criticize the speaker's delivery and interrupt the flow of what they are saying to ask questions.

- O Assume you already know what the issue is and how to resolve it.

Giving feedback

Getting feedback on our everyday actions in the form of positive and negative comments is what helps us grow and improve, both personally and professionally. But it needs to be delivered carefully and constructively to have the biggest impact. Understanding the situation and using the right words at the right time help increase the likelihood that what you say is of benefit.

When to give feedback

Good feedback doesn't just happen. It is the product of careful, deliberate communication strategies, coupled with good interpersonal communication skills. You can significantly increase the probability that the feedback you give helps others improve by understanding the role of feedback in both personal and professional settings.

Feedback is vital to any organization committed to improving itself because it is the only way for managers to know what needs to be improved. Giving and receiving feedback should be more than just a part of an employee's behavior; it should be a part of the whole organization's culture.

How to give feedback

Providing constructive, useful feedback involves more than simply responding to people as they speak to you. Consider the context in which the communication takes place, people's intentions as they speak (or choose not to speak), and your objectives as a manager.

BE BIAS-FREE

Before delivering feedback, ensure that **unconscious biases** relating to race, gender, age, class, sexuality, or disability are not affecting your **expectations** about someone's behavior or performance. Antibias training, and using objective criteria to judge competencies can help.

Tip

FOCUS ON BEHAVIOR
If you are giving negative feedback, defuse any hostility and **minimize the fear** felt by the other person by depersonalizing the conversation: focus your comments on the behavior involved, not the people.

In focus

LANGUAGE

Not everyone has the same understanding of language, and certain words, phrases, or terms that mean one thing to a manager may mean something very different to a person receiving feedback. It is important, therefore, that the language used for feedback is acceptable to the person being spoken to and appropriate for the circumstances. The words used must be clearly understood and agreed upon by both parties. Acronyms or company jargon are only acceptable if it is clear that both parties know what they mean. Successful managers make sure they know whether the person they are giving feedback to shares the same frame of reference they do, avoid language that will cause confusion, and choose words that are universally understood.

GIVE BOTH POSITIVE AND NEGATIVE FEEDBACK

People are more likely to **pay attention** to your complaints if they have also **received your compliments.** It is important to remember to tell people when they have done something well.

GET THE TIMING RIGHT

Before deciding to offer feedback, decide whether the **moment is right.** Constructive feedback can happen only within a **context of listening to** and **caring about** the other person. If the time isn't right, if the moment isn't appropriate, you can always delay briefly before offering your thoughts.

UNDERSTAND THE CONTEXT

This is the most important characteristic of feedback: find out where an event happened, why it happened, and what led up to it. Always **review the actions** and decisions that led up to the moment; never simply give feedback and leave.

Understanding nonverbal communication

Most of the meaning transferred from one person to another in a personal conversation comes not from the words that are spoken but from nonverbal signals. Learning to read, understand, and use these wordless messages isn't easy but is essential for effective communication.

Reading nonverbal signals

The movement, positioning, and use of the human body in various communication settings serve a number of functions:

- To highlight or emphasize some part of a verbal message
- To regulate the flow, pace, and back-and-forth nature of verbal messages
- To reinforce the general tone or attitude of a message
- To repeat what the verbal messages convey (holding up three fingers to indicate the number three, for example)
- To substitute for, or take the place of, verbal messages (such as giving a "thumbs-up" gesture)

Nonverbal cues are often difficult to read, especially because there are few body movements or gestures that have universally agreed-upon meanings. A colleague who looks tired or overworked to one person may appear disinterested or

> Body language can contradict the **verbal messages** being sent.

Using nonverbal signals

different to another. While looking for meaning in a particular movement, position, or gesture, be careful not to miss more important signals that reveal the true feelings of a speaker. Body language can sometimes contradict the verbal messages being sent. Tears in a person's eyes, for example, might involuntarily contradict a message telling you that the speaker is fine.

60%

to **65%** of **meaning** in social situations is conveyed **nonverbally.**

WATCH YOUR APPEARANCE
Make sure that your clothing and grooming are appropriate to your audience, your reasons for communicating, and the occasion.

RESTRAIN YOUR MOVEMENTS
Small gestures, close to your body, will convey an image of confidence and authority. Keep your voice low but audible and your posture relaxed.

TAKE CARE WITH TOUCH
The rules on touching others in a business context vary from culture to culture. Make sure you know and respect local customs.

WATCH YOUR EYE CONTACT
Eye contact usually reinforces trust; however, in some Asian cultures, looking a superior in the eye as you speak can be considered disrespectful.

USE VOCAL DYNAMICS
Tone, volume, rate, pitch, forcefulness, and enunciation all convey meaning about a subject and how you feel about the people in the room.

Running briefings and meetings

Briefings and meetings are an inescapable part of business life. They are a means of sharing information, initiating strategies, perpetuating a culture and building consensus around business goals. Done well, they're good for both business and morale, whether conducted in person or remotely.

Organizing a meeting

Be clear about the purpose of any meeting before you start planning. Invite only those people who are directly related to your goals and make sure you include all the key decision makers. Once you've arranged a time, place, and date that is convenient for everyone, send them all an agenda, making clear the meeting's theme and goals. In putting together the agenda, consider the following questions: What do we need to do in this meeting? What conversations will be important to those who attend? What information will we need to begin?

Prioritize the most important items so they will be discussed early in the meeting and assign a certain amount of time for each agenda item.

Giving a briefing

Briefing is a process by which you provide information to those who need it. As with any form of communication, think about your audience, your purpose and the occasion. Find out all you can about the audience and what they hope to take away from the session. State your purpose clearly and simply at the beginning of the meeting: "The purpose

ASK YOURSELF...
Do I need to call a meeting?

		YES	**NO**
1	Do I need to **motivate people**, giving them a "jump start" to get going?	☐	☐
2	Do I need to **share** general company or market **information** with people to help them do their jobs?	☐	☐
3	Do I need to **initiate a new program** or project?	☐	☐
4	Do I wish to **introduce people** to one another, so they can benefit from each other's experiences?	☐	☐

Case study

A COMPETITIVE ADVANTAGE
As CEO of the international retail giant Walmart, David Glass knew the company would have to be quick to deploy merchandising strategies, particularly in response to moves made by competitors. Each Saturday morning, when sales results for the week were transmitted to the corporate headquarters, Glass would gather key subordinates to share information from people in the field. They would tell the sales team what their competitors were doing; the senior team would then focus on corrective actions they wanted to take. By noon, regional managers would call district managers, and they would discuss and agree on the changes they would implement in the next week. "By noon on Saturday," Glass said, "we had all our corrections in place. Our competitors, for the most part, got their sales results on Monday for the week prior."

f this briefing is to look at budget rojections for the next 90 days." et them know why you're calling he meeting now.

Delivering a brief
When giving a briefing meeting, choose he delivery that best suits your speaking tyle and the needs of the audience. here are three forms to choose from:

- **Memorized presentations** These are delivered verbatim, just as you wrote them. This gives you total control over the material, but unless you're a trained actor, there's a risk that you'll sound wooden and the material contrived. Worse yet, you may forget where you are and have to start again or refer to notes.
- **Scripted briefings** These are more common, but they can also sound stilted. The problem with reading is that you risk losing eye contact by lowering your chin, and it also compresses your vocal pitch. If you do use a script, rehearse carefully and look up frequently, making regular eye contact with your audience.
- **Extemporaneous briefings** These are delivered either without notes or with visual aids to prompt your memory. They are the most effective choice, looking more spontaneous while actually being thoroughly researched, tightly organized, and well rehearsed.

Tip

ANTICIPATE QUESTIONS
Do your best to address audience concerns, questions, doubts, and fears in advance. **Plan the content** of your briefing around the needs of those in the audience.

Communicating to persuade

Whether you are trying to sell a product, convince your superiors to release more resources, convince an investor, or win a promotion, you need a clear strategy to persuade your audience. Removing the barriers to people saying "yes" is a two-way process.

Understanding the audience

Before you can expect your request to be understood and considered, you first need to understand your audience. What are their interests, their motivators, and their possible objections to your proposal? Most successful attempts at persuasion involve four separate, yet related, steps. Following these steps won't guarantee success with any particular audience, but they will set the stage for the attitudes you're trying to shape in your team and the behavior you hope will follow.

GETTING THEIR ATTENTION

If you want to motivate people to do something, you first have to catch their attention. Research shows that we **selectively choose** what to pay attention to, both as a defense mechanism against sensory overload and because we **seek out messages with particular value** for us. We ignore virtually everything else. There are two ways to capture attention:

- Use **physical stimuli,** such as bright lights, sound, motion, or color.
- Present stimuli that **relate directly to the needs** or goals of those you want to persuade.

PROVIDING A MOTIVATION

Next, you need to **provide a reason** for people to act. A persuasive writer or speaker is one who can **lead others to believe** in what he or she is advocating and then encourage some form of behavior in line with that belief. This amounts to giving good reasons for what you believe. These are not reasons you think are good but reasons your team thinks are good.

Identify the needs and interests of your team and connect them to your message. Which of their needs are you fulfilling? **Appeal to their sense of rationality**—show why it makes sense to act on your message. Or, **call on their sense of conformity** by showing how well others will view them if they act on your message.

When to use one- or two-sided arguments

ONE-SIDED ARGUMENT	TWO-SIDED ARGUMENT
The audience initially agrees with you, and your aim is simply to intensify support.	You suspect or know that the audience initially disagrees with your position.
The audience will not be exposed to any form of counter-persuasion.	You know the audience will be exposed to subsequent counter-persuasion.
The audience is not well informed or may become easily confused by an opponent's argument or evidence.	You hope to produce a more enduring result with a knowledgeable audience.

MOVING OTHERS TO ACT

Once you have captured the attention of those you want to persuade and have given them good cause to believe the message, you must provide them with a **clear channel for action.**

First, however, take time to **reassure them:** show them that there is a high probability that **you can deliver** on the promised reward. Your team needs to know that what you've promised will actually come true.

Next, **recommend a specific proposal or action.** Tell your team exactly what you want them to do, describe how you would like them to go about it, and set out a realistic time frame. Make sure that everyone on your team knows how and when **progress will be measured** and identify the end point and the rewards for achievement that lie ahead.

KEEPING THEM ON SIDE

The arguments that you use to persuade others can be one-sided, presenting your case alone, or two-sided, presenting your case as well as dealing with real and potential counterarguments. **Choose your approach** based on the knowledge and preconceptions of your audience. If you decide to use a two-sided argument, you should:

- **Warn your team** that others may try to change their minds.
- **State some opposing arguments** and then refute them. If you are aware of an opposing message, consider previewing at least part of it to the audience and then explaining why it is flawed.
- **Encourage commitment** in some tangible or visible way. It's more difficult for people to back away from positions for which they've publicly proclaimed their support.

Managing conflict

Conflict can arise from a variety of sources, but many experts see it as a function of such workplace issues as personality, personal and professional relationships, cultural differences, working environments, demands of the marketplace, and, of course, competition. As organizations increasingly use teamwork, differences between team members can lead to conflict.

LIMITED RESOURCES

Everything from office space to budgets may put people in competition with one another. Allocate scarce resources fairly to avoid this.

VALUES, GOALS, AND PRIORITIES

Confrontation can occur when people in an organization don't agree on strategic direction or basic priorities. Agreement on goals, large and small, can help avoid this.

Identifying the sources of conflict

Not all conflict within an organization is unhealthy, but conflict between and among people within an organization can quickly become counter-productive, divisive, and destructive if not properly managed. Conflict may develop over any number of issues or factors, but these five appear regularly:

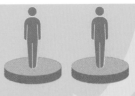

HUMAN DRIVE FOR SUCCESS

Conflicts can arise as a result of the natural sense of goal orientation that every human experiences. Some organizations actively foster a sense of competition among their members, creating many competitors and few rewards.

CHANGE

Many changes, including those to annual budgets, organizational priorities, lines of authority, or limits of responsibility, as well as restructuring, mergers, divestitures, and layoffs, can create anxiety, uncertainty, and conflict in an organization.

POORLY DEFINED RESPONSIBILITIES

Conflict may result from differences between formal job descriptions and the daily expectations of the role. Review and agree on who is responsible for what (and to whom).

Conflict resolution techniques

Resolving conflicts between team members is an important function of an effective manager. To begin the process, you should first ensure that both parties acknowledge that the conflict exists and the effects that it is having on team performance and morale. It may be that one party sees the problem as trivial or is ignoring the issue. Next, encourage the parties to set aside time to address the problem—schedule the first meeting and offer to participate in the process.

Get people to **agree on the small stuff** first: when this happens, the big issues become **easier to address.**

LISTEN CAREFULLY

Find out what's on people's minds and ask them what they're thinking and how they feel.

FOCUS ON INTERESTS

Focus not on a person's demands but on their interests—the reasons behind their demands.

RECOGNIZE FEELINGS

Accept feelings in others and work to communicate empathy. Keep your own emotions in check to ensure that you act professionally.

SEPARATE PEOPLE FROM PROBLEMS

Rather than saying, "I can't support you," say, "I'm not in favor of that solution."

KEEP COMMUNICATING

Keep the lines of communication open and speak as frankly and honestly as possible.

START SMALL

Get people to agree on the small stuff first. Once they start to agree on a few things, the big issues won't be as difficult.

Reconciling two sides

SUMMARIZE THE AGREEMENT

Review all the details with everyone involved. Make sure all are in agreement.

DEVISE OPTIONS

Find alternatives for mutual gain. By working together on the options, you can shift the dynamic from competition to cooperation.

CUT YOUR LOSSES

Sometimes the conflict has simply gone too far, and you must decide to make personnel changes.

FIND THE SOURCE

Track the conflict to its source. Don't accept the first answers you find; employees may have underlying concerns.

Communicating
externally

In today's global economy, you may find yourself communicating across companies, countries, and cultures, through a variety of media, including the internet. Focus on your company's core goals and identity to ensure consistent messaging.

04

Negotiating successfully

Negotiation is a process in which people attempt to persuade others to cooperate or assist in attaining outcomes that they value. The process often involves bargaining—giving up something in order to get something else—as well as collaboration, cooperation, and compromise.

Exploring interests

A key distinction to make in negotiating is recognizing the difference between interests and positions. A position is a hard line in the sand: a statement of a single acceptable outcome. Interests, on the other hand, are the reasons behind that position. Spend time seeing the negotiation from the other party's point of view; this may help you anticipate what is really important to them. This is key because there may be more than one way of meeting those interests. Can you find an alternative, workable position that will still satisfy the other party's interests as well as your own?

> Don't make a big **concession** right away—the other side may think there is a lot of **"give" in your position.**

Making the opening offer

If you have done your homework and have a good idea of the bargaining range, then you should make the opening offer. That offer anchors the bargaining process. Your opening offer should reflect your aspirations but not be ridiculous. If it is way out of range, you risk insulting the other party and damaging trust. If the other party makes the opening offer, and it is outrageous, don't discuss it. Simply dismiss it, indicate that it is not a possibility, and start again.

Your opening offer should leave you room to make concessions, but bear in mind that any you do make will provide the other party with information. If they make concessions, you should reciprocate, or they may view you with distrust and become more competitive. Don't make too large a concession right away, however, or the other side may think there is considerable "give" in your bargaining range.

Tip

CONSIDER COMPENSATION
Sometimes parties can be **enticed into an agreement** through the offer of something unrelated to the issues in negotiation. Think about **what might be valuable** to the other party but inexpensive for you to offer.

Recognizing significant points

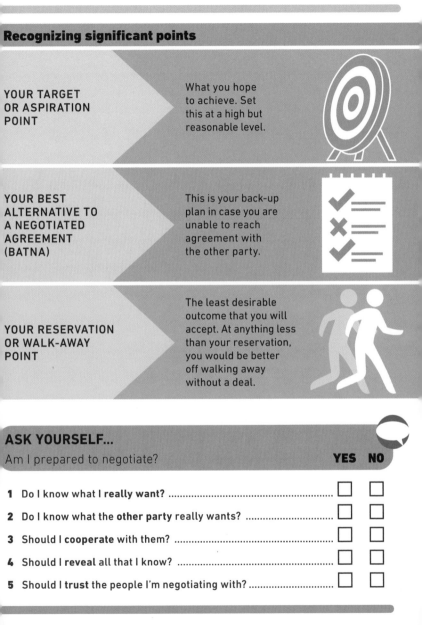

YOUR TARGET OR ASPIRATION POINT

What you hope to achieve. Set this at a high but reasonable level.

YOUR BEST ALTERNATIVE TO A NEGOTIATED AGREEMENT (BATNA)

This is your back-up plan in case you are unable to reach agreement with the other party.

YOUR RESERVATION OR WALK-AWAY POINT

The least desirable outcome that you will accept. At anything less than your reservation, you would be better off walking away without a deal.

ASK YOURSELF...

Am I prepared to negotiate?

	YES	NO
1 Do I know what I **really want**?	☐	☐
2 Do I know what the **other party** really wants?	☐	☐
3 Should I **cooperate** with them?	☐	☐
4 Should I **reveal** all that I know?	☐	☐
5 Should I **trust** the people I'm negotiating with?	☐	☐

Selling

Selling is both a form of persuasion and a process of relationship building. Most people don't want to feel as if they're being sold something; they would prefer to believe that they're buying it. This involves a balance of thoughtful questions, active listening, and a well-prepared presentation.

Prospecting and presenting

Selling involves actively looking for prospects who have the money, the authority, and a desire to buy. Before you contact a prospect, make sure that they fulfill these criteria and that you know both what you want to achieve and how. Develop a presentation that you can deliver confidently. This may be entirely memorized, formulaic (allowing some buyer–seller interaction), or entirely flexible and interactive. If you're offering a solution to a specific problem, base your proposal around a detailed analysis of the buyer's situation. Before you contact a prospect, always:

- Determine your call objectives. Are they specific, measurable, achievable, realistic, and well timed?
- Develop a customer profile. What do you know about the person who is making the buying decision?
- Familiarize yourself with all the customer benefits.
- Develop a sales presentation.

Develop a presentation that you can deliver **confidently.** It may be **memorized, formulaic,** or entirely flexible and **interactive.**

Closing the sale

First, ask the prospect's opinion about the benefits you're offering, using a question such as "How does this sound to you?" If this throws up any objections, handle them as they arise. Don't repeat negative statements or concerns; focus on positive outcomes. There are various ways to close a sale, so choose the one that is most appropriate to your situation.

Ways to close a sale

USE THE MINOR POINTS CLOSE

Ask the prospect to make **low-risk decisions** on minor, low-cost elements. Then, ask for the order.

Tip

Tip

MAKE A POSITIVE FIRST IMPRESSION
Be positive: smile, be enthusiastic, and open conversation with a **thoughtful compliment** or a **prediction** related to your product.

USE THE ASSUMPTIVE CLOSE
When the prospect is **close to a decision,** say, "I'll call your order in tonight."

GIVE AN ALTERNATIVE CHOICE
Give **two options** and then ask, "Which of these do you prefer?"

SUMMARIZE THE BENEFITS
Present the main **features, advantages,** and **benefits** and then ask for the order.

USE THE SCARCITY CLOSE
If true, tell the prospect that these items are **so popular,** there may not be many of them left.

USE THE CONTINUOUS "YES" CLOSE
Develop a **set of questions** the prospect will answer "yes" to and then ask for the order.

Communicating across countries and cultures

Advances in remote communications technology have brought unprecedented change across the globe. Video chat, instant messaging email, and other tools are allowing people living far apart to connect and collaborate efficiently and effectively. But even as the world comes closer together, each of us has retained something essential to our identity as humans: our culture.

Defining culture

Culture is everything that people have, think, and do as members of their society. Culture affects and is a central part of our economy and the organizations that employ us. It is composed of material objects, ideas, values, and attitudes as well as expected patterns of behavior. Whatever your business, you're likely to encounter people of different ethnicity, citizenship, and cultural origin. Dealing with people of different cultures, conducting business over international borders, traveling safely, and communicating effectively are not always easy but are essential for success in today's business world.

> Culture is composed of material **objects, ideas, values,** and **attitudes.**

Understanding culture

When you're communicating with a culture other than your own, you need to **be sensitive** about the particular beliefs and values of that culture and how they differ from your own.

CULTURE IS INGRAINED

Few of us would give a moment's thought to learning how to be a part of the culture we have grown up in. Our first culture is so **closely defined** for each of us that we're barely aware that we have one. Learning a second culture, though takes a **purposeful effort.**

Recognizing change

The culture of any country is constantly undergoing change. The clothing people wear, the transportation they use, the books they read, the topics they talk about, and so on—all change over time. This is due to the internal forces of discovery, invention, and innovation and external forces, including the diffusion of ideas from other cultures. Some cultures change fast, while others evolve more slowly, either by preference or because they are more physically isolated. Changes in culture are often reflected in changes in the way people speak and write; make sure that your own communications reflect these changes.

Tip

INVESTIGATE THE SUBCULTURES
Virtually all large, complex cultures contain subcultures. These are small groups of people with **separate** and **specialized interests**—essentially, they are niche markets.

CULTURE IS UNIVERSAL

All societies have an interest in passing along values and norms to their children, thereby creating and **defining a culture.** No matter where you travel, you'll find people with cultures that differ from the one in which you grew up; noticing these differences will **strengthen your communications.**

CULTURES ALLOCATE VALUES

Some cultures **engage in behaviors** that others might consider reprehensible. Be careful never to cause offense when communicating by inadvertently breaking taboos or talking about matters that are considered "off limits."

Communicating internationally

On a personal level, communicating across international borders means becoming more aware of the ways in which your thinking or actions are culturally biased.

Start by recognizing that your own education, background, and beliefs may be considered fine or even laudable in your own culture, but they may not count for much to someone from a different country. Take a nonjudgmental position toward those from other cultures, and you are likely to find that they will extend the same hospitable tolerance toward you. If you find yourself making personal judgments, keep them to yourself. When you're writing or speaking to people from another culture, try to understand life from their perspective. Learn to communicate respect for other people's ways, their country, and their values.

Tip

LEARN TO RECOGNIZE "NO"
Some cultures consider it rude to say "no." If you are met with vague answers to requests, such as **"I'll try"** or **"yes, but it may be difficult,"** in these cultures, it may be safer to assume that your request has been refused.

In focus

ETHNOCENTRISM

All cultures, to one degree or another, display ethnocentrism: the tendency to evaluate a foreigner's behavior by the standards of one's own culture and to believe that one's culture is superior to all others. We tend to take our own culture for granted. We're born into it, and we live with its rules and assumptions day in and day out. We quickly come to believe that the way we live is simply "the way things should be." As a result, we often see our behavior as correct. However, culture is not value-neutral. We have good reasons for believing and behaving as we do, but that doesn't necessarily mean that others are "wrong."

Adopting the right attitude

You don't have to adopt the local culture and begin doing things the way they do. Just be aware and respect that they do things differently. "Your way" of communicating might work wonderfully in your own culture but less well in another. Try to adopt an open-minded approach, focusing on:

- **Developing a tolerance for ambiguity** Accept the fact that you'll never understand everything about another culture. However, you can still appreciate and function within that culture satisfactorily.
- **Becoming more flexible** Things won't always go the way you want. A small degree of flexibility will prove enormously helpful.
- **Practicing a little humility** Acknowledge what you do not know or understand. Because you weren't raised in another's culture (or may not even speak the language well), you'll never fully understand all aspects of it. Displaying humility and acceptance will win friends, influence people, and make life easier. Communication consists of the transfer of meaning, so do everything you can to make sure that your messages are not misunderstood.

ASK YOURSELF...

Do I understand the culture?

YES   NO

1 Do I understand the **basic business etiquette** of introductions and meetings in this new culture? .... ☐ ☐

2 Do I know how to recognize the **key decision makers** within a group? .... ☐ ☐

3 Am I familiar with the culture's **business dress code**? .... ☐ ☐

4 Do I know how many **languages are spoken** and which is the **official language**? .... ☐ ☐

5 Have I learned the preferred **forms of negotiation**? .... ☐ ☐

6 Do I know which **forms of media** are popular among which demographic groups? .... ☐ ☐

Writing for the web

The way that people read a website is different than the way in which they read other information. You must take this into account when developing web content. It is not sufficient to simply repurpose content written for print; you need to write specifically for the internet, thinking carefully about what your audience needs and what you want them to know.

Engaging your readers

Why is writing for the internet different? First, people rarely read websites word-for-word. Instead, they scan the page, picking out individual words and sentences. Rather than starting at the beginning of a page and reading from start to finish, internet readers will scan a site, looking for relevant items, and then if they find something useful, save it for later reference. Guide your reader by highlighting the most important or useful points in your document with headings, lists, and eye-catching typography.

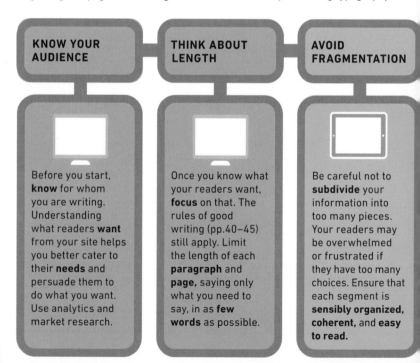

KNOW YOUR AUDIENCE

Before you start, **know** for whom you are writing. Understanding what readers **want** from your site helps you better cater to their **needs** and persuade them to do what you want. Use analytics and market research.

THINK ABOUT LENGTH

Once you know what your readers want, **focus** on that. The rules of good writing (pp.40–45) still apply. Limit the length of each **paragraph** and **page,** saying only what you need to say, in as **few words** as possible.

AVOID FRAGMENTATION

Be careful not to **subdivide** your information into too many pieces. Your readers may be overwhelmed or frustrated if they have too many choices. Ensure that each segment is **sensibly organized, coherent,** and **easy to read.**

16%

f users read a web page **word-for-word;** most people nly **scan** the text, picking out **ighlighted words,** bold or olored **section headings,** nd bulleted points.

Navigation aids

Web readers generally do not read pages in sequence. Instead, they jump around on a website, looking for content that interests them, navigating back and forth across images, ideas, and words. Providing information in precise segments or "chunks" will allow readers to quickly find what they're looking for. A well-constructed chunk provides readers with a comprehensive account as well as links to related or supporting pages. When your content lends itself to such treatment, use lists rather than paragraphs. Readers can pick out information more easily from a list than from a fully developed paragraph.

ENSURE EASY NAVIGATION	BE ACCESSIBLE	MAKE IT EASY TO FIND
Your main goal is to **provide access** to the information people are most likely to want. Provide **easy-to-follow clues** that lead to chunks of useful information. Include brief but **comprehensive summaries** of longer documents.	Make your content accessible. Help visually impaired readers by ensuring your pages are screen-reader friendly, with clear headings, links, and image descriptions. Want to attract international visitors? Consider translating pages.	**Make it easy** for readers to find and save information. Research keywords and craft metadata (page descriptions) to make pages more visible on search engines. If aspects of your content are lengthy, try **linking to a** downloadable **PDF** file.

Communicating through social media

Social media channels on the internet—such as Facebook, Twitter, Instagram, TikTok, YouTube, and LinkedIn—have transformed the way people do business. A social media presence is no longer an option but an essential—people of all ages are influenced in their buying decisions by a brand's presence on social media. So, how do you maximize the impact of your social media output?

Devise a strategy

Social media can be used in many different ways—from increasing awareness of your company's brand, increasing traffic to your website, and forging new business contacts at home and abroad to boosting sales or attracting customers. So, the first decision you should make is to set the purpose of your social media interaction. Be specific in your goals and list them in order of importance.

Next, carry out some research—formal or informal— into the internet habits of your customers or target audience: Who are they? Which social media channels do they use? What do they expect from these channels? You will have far more success if you tune in to the needs of your customers.

Also keep in mind that reaching a sizable social media audience nowadays involves more than simply posting content. You will likely need to invest in paid-for advertising, as paying the social media platform to show your posts to a wider audience will give them a better chance of generating the impact you want.

Focus on success

Always consider how your social media activities will translate into business growth—there is little point in maintaining a costly presence on social channels if it doesn't affect the bottom line. Think about how you can measure the effectiveness of your activities. Having a large number of followers on Facebook or Twitter, for example, may be impressive but may be of little value if it fails to translate into improved business performance. Similarly, building up many connections on LinkedIn may be of little use if you fail to leverage these connections to create

73%

of marketers say acquiring **new customers** is their biggest **social media** goal.

Three major uses of social media

	CREATIVE BRANDING	BUILDING A COMMUNITY	CUSTOMER SERVICE
ACTIVITIES	O Posting entertaining content in a variety of media. O Creating compelling stories. O Using humor helps boost engagement.	O Creating a space where people with a common interest can interact. O Providing useful information and resources for your community.	O Engaging with customer queries and solving their problems. O Measuring customers' sentiments toward your business.
REMEMBER TO	O Keep your brand message, tone of voice, and writing style consistent across all platforms and interactions.	O Keep your content lively, current, and varied. Just giving links to other websites will not encourage repeat visits from others.	O Set up a separate account for this purpose and ensure that your responses are quick and authoritative.

ew business. Always consider how ou'll gauge the value of the effort you vest in social media.

Remember, too, what social media —social. Too many companies use it s a one-way form of communication, ke a corporate website, and fail to vite user comments or contributions. he more dialogue you can build with our customers, the more effective our use of social channels will be.

ngaging with your audience

ow you communicate through social edia channels depends on your oals. However, you should always:

- Post regularly: a media stream to which you contribute sporadically will soon dry up.
- Post different types of content: the written word is not enough to engage your audience. Post high-quality images and videos too.
- Post interesting comments: try to encourage debate, comments, or likes rather than making passive statements.
- Vary contributors for differing perspectives.
- Always respond to posts from users within a reasonable time frame.

Running a video meeting

Improvements in technology have made video conferencing an essential tool for many businesses. While video-chat apps, such as Skype and Zoom, are easy to use, it is vital to plan carefully to avoid technical hitches and make the experience rewarding and successful for those involved.

Preparing a video meeting

With more people working remotely, online meetings are increasingly common, allowing dispersed colleagues to connect face-to-face and encouraging a sense of unity. Running a productive video meeting depends largely on the time you spend preparing for it. Start by deciding what you want your meeting to achieve and devise a plan accordingly, taking into account issues such as technical requirements, group size, timings, and materials.

Plan your video meeting

Choose your technology and make sure you and your participants are comfortable using it. For conference-style sessions, consider using a specific webinar tool.

Identify the purpose of the video meeting: explain to people what they will be doing and why.

Plan the agenda; don't just try to "wing it" as you go along. Place easily accomplished items first on the list.

Identify a chairperson who will be responsible for starting, stopping, and running the meeting.

CHAIRING A VIDEO MEETING

Do's	Don'ts
○ **Ask people to give their names, titles, and locations.**	○ Introduce some of the participants, but ignore others.
○ **Keep to the agenda and stay on time.**	○ Introduce new items not agreed to in advance.
○ **Take control and provide people with opportunities to speak.**	○ Allow people to talk with one another in side conversations.
○ **Take notes of what is being said and by whom.**	○ Fail to capture what's been said and agreed to.

Video meetings are increasingly common, allowing dispersed colleagues to connect **face-to-face** and encouraging a sense of **unity.**

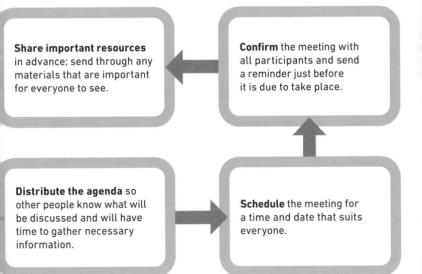

Share important resources in advance; send through any materials that are important for everyone to see.

Confirm the meeting with all participants and send a reminder just before it is due to take place.

Distribute the agenda so other people know what will be discussed and will have time to gather necessary information.

Schedule the meeting for a time and date that suits everyone.

Looking presentable

On the day, dress conservatively: avoid busy patterns, thin stripes, and small prints that draw attention. Act always as if people are watching you and refrain from quirky mannerisms—these may go unnoticed in a meeting but are magnified in a video call. Sit up straight, pay attention, and project a professional image. Make sure you know where the camera lens is before you start the call—it is not always above the screen. Make sure to look directly at the camera lens when you are speaking. You'll enhance your credibility dramatically if you focus squarely on the camera; others will think you're speaking directly to them.

Ensure the room from which you are calling is **tidy** and that there's nothing distracting in the **background.**

Pay particular attention to the lighting in the room, making sure that **your face is well lit;** try placing a large sheet of white paper flat on the desk in front of you to **reduce any harsh shadows** on your face.

Try moving your computer's video camera closer to you so that your **head and upper shoulders** occupy the whole screen—any smaller and it becomes difficult to see and read your facial expressions.

Succeeding with video calls

Today's computer-based video-conferencing systems, such as Zoom, Microsoft Teams, and Skype, put the power to run virtual meetings in the hands of anyone with a laptop and an internet connection. However, with that power comes the responsibility of looking after every aspect of the call. Follow a few simple technical and presentation tips to make your online meetings more professional and productive.

Add another light behind you to illuminate the room and provide a sense of place.

Consider **recording the meeting** (but ask permission first).

Close other programs on your computer—especially if they make a noise (email clients, for example).

Check what the other person **can see** before you call.

Look into the camera, not at your picture on the screen.

Take some time to **get to know the platform's controls** so that you can, for example, mute the microphone or share you screen, if necessary.

Switch off any potential distractions, such as the telephone, and set your status to "**Do not disturb**" so that you won't get interrupted by other incoming calls.

Use gestures and expressions to **emphasize** your words.

Sounding good

Once you are connected, avoid unguarded comments—assume someone may be watching and listening. Speak a bit more slowly than usual to ensure that everyone understands you and use gestures and facial expressions to emphasize your words. Don't read a speech, but keep summarizing key issues as you move along. Refer to the agenda and remind people of elapsed time as you move from point to point. In larger meetings, get participants to submit questions via the video app's chat function or a shared document to avoid interruptions. At the end, summarize the issues discussed and agreed to. After the event, prepare and distribute minutes within a few days.

Communicating in a crisis

There is a huge difference between business problems and crises. Problems are commonplace in business. A crisis, on the other hand, is a major, unpredictable event. Without careful communication, crises have the potential to damage an organization's reputation and financial standing, together with those of its employees, shareholders, products, and services.

Identifying the crisis

Some business crises can be prepared for (to a certain extent), while others require an immediate and creative response. There are two main types:

- **Internal crises** These arise within the company, such as accounting scandals or labor strikes.
- **External crises** These are caused by an external factor, such as the COVID-19 pandemic, a natural or technological disaster, or external threats by special-interest groups.

It is important to recognize the type of crisis you are facing, as this will help you pinpoint the groups of people you will need to communicate with and give you an idea of how fast and how far the effects of the crisis could potentially spread.

> Assemble an effective **team** and isolate its members from other **day-to-day concerns.**

Case study

L'ORÉAL

French cosmetics company L'Oréal had spent several years expanding its digital operations before the COVID-19 pandemic. But when the crisis hit in 2020, it decided to go all in. Whereas some rivals reacted to the downturn in the beauty market by stripping back marketing, L'Oréal kept communications open online, investing 77 percent of its media budget into digital. As well as letting people know about its efforts to donate hand sanitizer and financial aid, the company also sought to forge stronger relationships with customers, encouraging them to ask questions and order online. "Social distancing? Yes. Social media distancing? No," as one of its online posts put it. The results were clear: a 62 percent growth in e-commerce in 2020. "We did in eight weeks what it took three years to do, doubling e-commerce from 18 percent of our business to 34 percent at the peak in April," said then chief digital officer Lubomira Rochet.

ealing with a crisis

ommunicating in a crisis is different om managing a business problem. ou are likely to be unprepared, have sufficient information, and be under me pressure. Crisis communication often offers few precedents to work from and intense scrutiny from outside the organization. This can lead to a loss of control and a sense of panic, so it is important to remain calm and address the crisis systematically.

Addressing a crisis

WHAT TO DO	HOW TO DO IT
01 **Get information**	O Deal from an informed position and separate fact from rumor. Document what you know and don't know for sure. Become the source of reliable information and keep the information flowing. O Determine the real problem in the short term and the long term. Check whether this is really your problem.
02 **Put people in place**	O Put someone in charge. Give them responsibility, authority, and the resources to get the job done. Tell people who it is. O Assemble an effective but nimble team. Staff it with the expertise needed and provide resources. Isolate team members from other day-to-day concerns.
03 **Draw up a plan**	O Develop a strategy, which should include ways to resolve the problem, deal with affected parties, and communicate both today and in the long term. O Establish goals. Define your objectives for the short term, mid-term, and long term. Measure relentlessly and don't be discouraged by critics, negative press, or short-term failures.
04 **Start communicating**	O Centralize communications. Incoming communication provides intelligence, while outgoing communication gives a degree of control over what is being said about the situation. O Rely on a strictly limited number of spokespersons who are knowledgeable, authoritative, responsive, patient, and good humored.

Dealing with the media

Being the subject of a news media interview is never easy and can be stressful and risky. You might say the wrong thing or forget to say what's most important about the subject of the interview, or your comments might be taken out context when they're aired. However, by following a few basic rules, you can limit risk and use the interview to your advantage.

Capitalizing on opportunity

Learn to see media interviews as an opportunity to reach a large audience. They represent a chance to tell your story and to inform the public of your business or expertise. They also offer an opportunity to address public concerns and set the record straight, if you're the subject of misinformation in the press. They can be a forum in which to apologize if you've done something wrong and a chance to reinforce the credibility of your organization and its leadership. Don't feel bullied into giving an interview if you're not ready: you can say "no" or delegate to another staff member who is more accustomed to dealing with the media.

Never feel bullied into **giving an interview** if you're not ready: you can say "no" or **delegate** the task.

Preparing for an interview

The best way to **ensure a good interview** is thorough preparation.

Gather all the **information** you will need. Make sure you know the latest **facts and figures**.

Research the reporter; deal only with **established,** professional journalists.

CHECKLIST...

Succeeding in media interviews   YES   NO

1 Are you clear about **what you hope to achieve**
   from the interview? .... ☐   ☐

2 Do you know **which items of information** you can share
   and which are confidential? .... ☐   ☐

3 Have you decided on a method for **avoiding arguments**
   if the reporter provokes you? .... ☐   ☐

4 Do you know **how to respond** to false allegations without
   repeating the phrases the reporter uses? .... ☐   ☐

5 Are you focused on remaining **professional and likable**,
   no matter what happens in the interview? .... ☐   ☐

Gather all the information
you will need: make sure
that you have the latest
facts and figures.

Tip

**GET YOUR POINT
IN EARLY**
A reporter may not ask the
one question you're most
hoping to talk about. **Raise
the issue** yourself, **get your
points in,** and **repeat them
frequently.** Use the free
air time or print space to
your benefit.

Ask your
Public Affairs
or Corporate
Communication
office for **help**
and **guidance.**

Find out the
**subject and
background** of
the story and
ask who else is
participating.

Double-check
the **time, date,**
and **location** of
the interview.

Building brands

Communicating the essence of a brand is more than simply using words and visuals to convey an image. This is because a brand is both a process and a product. It's a living, breathing organism that must be nurtured and protected if it is to survive and thrive.

Winning hearts and minds

A brand is, first of all, a promise of an experience. It is what a product, service, or company stands for in the minds of customers and prospects. At its very core, a brand is a perception or a feeling. It's the feeling evoked when we think about a product or the company that delivers it. And, of course, a brand is the basis for differentiation in the marketplace—a way to separate yourself from all other competitors in the hearts and minds of your customers.

Defining the brand

The most crucial characteristics of a brand are content and consistency. To succeed, a brand must make a clear and unambiguous promise to its stakeholders (customers, employees, investors, suppliers, creditors, and others) and then deliver on that promise.

The Starbucks brand, for example, is clearly aligned with the customer experience. When regulars in Starbucks' coffee shops began to complain about the smell of hot breakfast sandwiches, former CEO Howard Schultz decided to focus on the core experiences (and aromas) of freshly ground coffee and a relaxing environment. Electronics giant Samsung's brand promise is "Do what you can't." It encapsulates the firm's desire to be at the forefront of technology, enabling people to do things that have only just become possible.

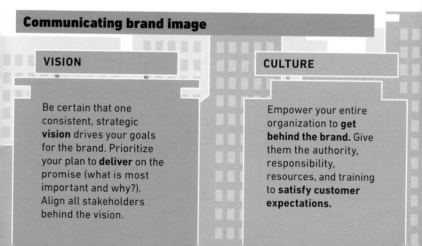

Communicating brand image

VISION

Be certain that one consistent, strategic **vision** drives your goals for the brand. Prioritize your plan to **deliver** on the promise (what is most important and why?). Align all stakeholders behind the vision.

CULTURE

Empower your entire organization to **get behind the brand.** Give them the authority, responsibility, resources, and training to **satisfy customer expectations.**

In focus

BRAND VALUE

Brands that have a clear sense of themselves and have worked diligently to deliver on their promises are often quite durable, withstanding economic down-turns, changes in customer preferences, and game-changing innovations in their product category. The value of developing brands is highlighted in a quote by John Stuart, former CEO of Quaker Oats Company: "If this company were split up, I would gladly give you the property, plant, and equipment, and I would take the brands and trademarks . . . and I would fare better than you." Swedish furniture giant IKEA has taken this idea of brand–infrastructure separation to heart, building it into its corporate structure. While its stores and operations are owned by one group, INGKA Holding, its brand and trademarks are owned by another, Inter IKEA Holding.

ACTION

Specify and communicate those actions that are **essential to brand success** to those within the organization who must deliver on the promise.

VALUE

Consistently and continually **measure results.** Show your investors, associates, and business partners what you've accomplished and what improvements you have yet to make.

INNOVATION

You cannot stand still; you must **continually innovate** to stay ahead of the demands of the marketplace and the shifts in everything from demographics to target-group tastes and preferences. Demonstrate that you are both innovative and protective of the brand experience.

A **brand** helps separate you from your competitors in the **hearts and minds** of your customers.

Index

Acknowledgments

Stats

p.16 *Capitalizing on Effective Communication: How Courage, Innovation and Discipline Drive Business Results in Challenging Times 2009/2010*, Tower Watson

p.19 "Your Scarcest Resource," Michael Mankins, Chris Brahm, and Greg Caimi, *Harvard Business Review*, May 2014

p.32 "The Facts on How People Create Presentations—Based on Real-World Survey Data," Presentationpanda.com, 2018

p.35 "Do Your Slides Pass the Glance Test?," Nancy Duarte, *Harvard Business Review*, October 22, 2012

p.41 "Bad Writing Is Destroying Your Company's Productivity," Josh Bernoff, *Harvard Business Review*, September 6, 2016

p.56 "The Discipline of Listening," Ram Charan, *Harvard Business Review*, June 21, 2012

p.61 "Nonverbal Signals," Judee K. Burgoon in *Handbook of Interpersonal Communication*, Mark L. Knapp and Gerald R. Miller (Eds.), SageEditors, 1994

p.81 "How Users Read on the Web," Jakob Nielsen, Nielsen Norman Group, September 30, 1997

p.82 *Social Trends 2021*, Hootsuite

Publisher's acknowledgments
Delhi Team
Senior DTP Designer: Vishal Bhatia
Desk Editor: Saumya Agarwal

Second edition:
Senior Art Editor Gillian Andrews
Project Editor Hugo Wilkinson
Editor Marek Walisiewicz
Designers Paul Reid, Rebecca Johns
US Editors Margaret Parrish, Jill Hamilton
Managing Editor Gareth Jones
Senior Managing Art Editor Lee Griffiths
Production Editor Nikoleta Parasaki
Production Controller Mandy Inness
Jacket Designer Mark Cavanagh
Design Development Manager Sophia M.T.T.

Delhi Team:
Senior Editorial Manager Rohan Sinha
Deputy Managing Art Editor Sudakshina Basu

First edition:
Senior Editor Peter Jones
Senior Art Editor Helen Spencer
Executive Managing Editor Adèle Hayward
Managing Art Editor Kat Mead
Art Director Peter Luff
Publisher Stephanie Jackson
Production Editor Ben Marcus
Production Controller Hema Gohil
US Editor Margaret Parrish

First edition produced for
Dorling Kindersley Limited by
Cobalt id
www.cobaltid.co.uk